MONEY

Andrew Murray in Modern English

The Complete Classic

Updated for Today

Translated by Pastor Joe Lighthall

First published in 1897 by Fleming Revell Co.

The source text is in the public domain but this translation and accompanying editorial materials constitute original intellectual property © 2025 by Pastor Joe Lighthall.

Permission is required for reuse, reproduction, or distribution of this translated edition.

All rights reserved.

ISBN 978-1-918219-46-3

First Edition: December 2025

Published by: Cosmic Jive Publishing
www.cosmicjivepublishing.com
For permissions and inquiries, contact:
info@cosmicjivepublishing.com

WHY THIS BOOK NEEDED A FRESH VOICE

Andrew Murray's *Money* is, quite simply, one of the most searching, convicting, and life-changing books ever written on the subject of money and the kingdom of God.

It does what dozens of modern books on finances and generosity rarely manage: it lifts money out of the realm of budgets and bank accounts and places it squarely at the foot of the Cross. Murray shows, with relentless biblical clarity, that the way we handle money is one of the truest tests of whether the grace of the Lord Jesus—who became poor that we might become rich—has truly taken hold of our hearts.

Pastors, missionaries, and ordinary believers have testified for more than a century that this little book changed their entire view of possessions, giving, and discipleship. It has quietly shaped movements of radical generosity around the world.

Yet most people today never finish it.

The reason is not the message; the message is electric.

The barrier is the packaging: long, winding Victorian paragraphs, sentences that run for many lines, and many words that have faded from everyday use. Even readers with university degrees and years of Bible study often find themselves re-reading the same paragraph three times, losing the thread, and finally setting the book aside—robbed of the very blessing God intended for them.

That is why this new edition exists.

Every word of Murray's original argument is here—nothing added, nothing removed, nothing softened. The Scriptures he quoted remain in the form he used. The only thing that has changed is the delivery: clear, contemporary English and shorter sentences and paragraphs that let the truth land with the force Murray meant it to have.

Now a new generation can read without stumbling. Busy parents, young professionals, students, pastors preparing sermons, small-group leaders—anyone who has ever thought, "I know this book is powerful, but I just can't get through the old language—can finally meet the real Andrew Murray. And when they do, they discover that his words, once unlocked, burn as brightly and challenge as sharply as the day they were written.

My hope is that this fresh voice will do exactly what Murray's message what a fresh wind does to a sail: carry it farther, faster, and deeper into hearts that are hungry for the riches of Christ.

May the same Holy Spirit who inspired the original now use these updated words to set thousands more free from the love of money and free for the love of God.

Pastor Joe Lighthall, Dec. 2025

A Brief Note from the Editor

Every chapter, every section, every biblical quotation is here in the same order as the original. **Nothing has been removed, added, or softened.** What has changed is only the presentation:

- The Victorian-era language has been carefully rewritten in clear, contemporary English so today's readers can immediately grasp Murray's full message.
- Roman numerals have been replaced with ordinary numbers.
- Long, dense paragraphs have been broken into shorter ones for modern eyes
- A handful of brief notes have been added solely to explain historical references or rare terms no longer in everyday use.
- All Bible quotations are retained in the wording Murray himself used, because those precise shades of meaning matter.

The meaning, the challenge, and the power of the original words remain exactly the same — only now they are easier to read, to share and to apply.

PART 1
CHRIST'S VIEW OF MONEY

"Jesus beheld how the people cast money into the treasury: and many that were rich cast in much. And a certain poor widow came, and cast in a farthing. Jesus called His disciples, and saith unto them, This poor widow hath cast more in than all: for all they did cast in of their abundance; but she of her want did cast in all that she had, even all her living."—Mark 12. 41.

[Jesus sat opposite the temple treasury and observed people putting money into the offering boxes. He watched as many rich people contributed large sums, and then a poor widow came and put in two small copper coins—translated as 'farthing' in the version Andrew Murray references—Ed.]

Andrew Murray

In all our Christian life and Bible study, nothing is more important than learning the mind of Christ—thinking as He thought, feeling as He felt. There is no question that concerns us, no situation that ever arises, in which His words do not offer us guidance.

Today we want to understand Christ's mind about money—what He thought of it, and how He wants us to think and act just as He would do.

This is not easy. We are surrounded by the world's influence, and we easily fear becoming "impractical" if we think and act exactly as Christ did. But we must not be concerned. If we truly want to discover His will, He will guide us. We only need to honesty say to ourselves: I want to have Christ teach me how to keep and use my money.

Picture Jesus for a moment sitting by the temple treasury, watching people put in their offerings. We often associate thoughts about money in church with Judas or some hardworking deacon, or the treasurer or collector of some charitable society.

But see here - Jesus Himself watching the collection. As Jesus watches, He weighs each gift with God's scales and assigns it its true value.

He still does this in heaven today—not a single offering to God's work, large or small, escapes His notice. He measures its worth for the blessing it may bring now or what it may bring in eternity.

And He is willing to show us even now, in a quiet and listening heart, what He thinks of our giving.

Giving money is part of our spiritual life, watched over by Christ, and must be guided by His Word.

Let us try and discover what Scripture teaches about money.

Andrew Murray

1. MONEY-GIVING IS A CLEAR TEST OF CHARACTER.

In the world, money is the standard of value. It is difficult to say all that money means to the world. It represents labor and enterprise and cleverness. It is often a sign of God's blessing on hard work. It can purchase property, comfort, luxury, influence, and power. No wonder the world loves it, pursues it above everything, and often worships it. No wonder a man is so often judged and valued by how much he owns.

But it is not only in the kingdom of this world that a man is judged by his money. In the kingdom of God too, a man is judged by his money. However, in a different way.

The world asks, "What does a man own?" Christ asks, "How does he use what he has?"

When a man gives, the world asks, "How much did he give?" Christ asks, "How did he give it?" The world looks at the amount;

Money

Christ looks at the motive.

We can see this in the story of the poor widow. The rich gave large sums, but from their plenty, their surplus—giving which cost them nothing, that involved no sacrifice, that did not touch their level of comfort. There was no special love or devotion to God in it —their giving was only part of an easy, traditional religion.

But the widow gave a farthing and though a mere pittance, it was everything she had. She held nothing back. She gave all. Her gift won Christ's heart because it reflected His own self-giving love.

How different our standard is and Christ's is. We ask, "How much did she give?" Christ asks, "How much did she keep?" She kept nothing. We look at the gift. Christ asks whether the gift was a sacrifice.

The widow kept nothing over, she gave everything; the gift won Jesus' heart and approval, for it was in the spirit of His own self-sacrifice, who, being rich, became poor for our own sakes. The rich—out of their abundance—gave a lot: She, out of her need —gave all that she had.

You may ask if Christ wanted us all to give away everything, why didn't He then command it clearly in His word? You want a command to make you give everything but that would just be the spirit of the world in the church looking at what we give again, at our giving all. And that is just what Christ does not want and that He will not have.

He wants love, not compulsion. He desires willing, joyful, unforced giving. He wants every gift to be a gift warm and full of love, a true free will offering.

If you want the Master's approval like the poor widow did, remember one thing: you must put everything at His feet, to consider all you own as His— and to give as the natural outflow of a heart that loves God and others, a heart like Mary's that cannot help giving, just because it loves.

All my money giving—what a test of character! Lord Jesus, give me grace to love You deeply, so I may know how to give.

2. MONEY-GIVING IS A GREAT MEANS OF SPIRITUAL GROWTH.

Christ called His disciples to come and listen while He talked to them about the giving He saw in the temple. This was to guide his disciples' giving and ours. Our giving, if we listen to Christ with a real desire to learn, will have more influence on our spiritual growth than we realize.

The world's spirit is "the lust of the flesh, the lust of the eye, and the pride of life." Money is the great tool the world uses to satisfy its desires. But Christ says of His people, "They are not of the world, even as I am not of the world." We must show by our use of money that we are guided by heavenly principles, not worldly ones. In our spending, we must show that the spirit of heaven teaches us how to use money.

The Spirit of Heaven teaches us to use money for things that last for eternity and please God. "They that are Christ's have crucified the flesh with its desires." One powerful way to keep the crucifixion of the flesh real and active in our daily lives is to stop spending money on things that simply feed our selfish desires and comforts, and instead deliberately direct that same money toward the things that matter to God.

The way to conquer every temptation to spend money on the flesh is to have the heart filled with thoughts of the spiritual power of money. If you want to keep the flesh crucified, refuse to spend a penny on gratifying it. As much as money spent on self may nourish and strengthen and comfort self, money sacrificed to God may help the soul in the victory that overcomes both the world and the flesh.

The way we handle money can greatly strengthen our entire life of faith. Most people are constantly busy earning it—by its very nature, money tends to weigh the heart down and tie it firmly to earthly things, for it is the very lifeblood of this world.

This easily ties the heart to earth. It is faith that can give us continual victory over this temptation.

Every thought of the danger of money, every effort to resist it, every loving gift to God, helps our life of faith. We view all things in the light of God. We judge them from the perspective of eternity, and the money that passes through our hands, when devoted to God, can become a daily schooling in faith and heavenly-mindedness.

Giving away our money can do something truly special: it can strengthen our capacity to love.

Every spiritual gift grows stronger when we

actually use it—and this is especially true of love.

If we really understood this, we'd see that money is one of the best tools God gives us to grow love in our hearts. Every time we stop to think about someone else's need, feel compassion, and then open our hands to help, love is being exercised by us and stretched.

Each request for financial help and each generous response we give can awaken new love inside us and draw us into a deeper, happier surrender to the beautiful demands of loving others.

Giving your money generously can be one of the most powerful ways God pours His grace into your life and how you grow spiritually.

Each time you give, it's like a fresh, ongoing conversation with Him: you keep handing your whole life back to God, surrendering your all to Him, and in that simple act you show how seriously you want to follow Him—living in self-denial with open hands, trusting faith, and real and growing love.

3. Money-giving is a wonderful power for God.

What an amazing religion Christianity is! It takes money—the very symbol of this world's power, loaded with selfishness, greed, and pride—and transforms it into a tool for serving God and bringing Him glory.

Think of the poor. A small, loving gift of money, given at just the right moment, can bring real help and joy to tens of thousands of people who have no other way out.

God deliberately allows some to have more and others to have less, and here's one big reason why: just as buying and selling creates healthy interdependence in society, the giving and receiving of generous help creates countless opportunities for the deep happiness that comes from doing good and being cared for.

That's why Jesus said, "It is more blessed to give than to receive."

What an incredible, almost God-like privilege it is to have money in your hands and use it to lift someone out of need or put real joy on a poor person's face!

What a beautiful faith Christianity is—it turns the money we give away into something that brings us even greater happiness than the money we spend on ourselves.

The cash we spend on our own comfort usually just buys things that don't last and feed our earthly desires. But the money we give in love carries eternal weight, and it creates a double joy: deep gladness for the person who receives it, and an even richer happiness for the one who gives.

Think of the church and everything it does

in the world: missions at home and overseas, plus the thousands of ministries that help pull people out of sin and bring them to God and a life of holiness.

Is it really possible that ordinary money—when you give it with faith and love—gets transformed? That when you drop it into God's treasury with the right heart, heaven stamps it with eternal value and uses it to "purchase" real spiritual blessings?

Yes, it's absolutely true.

Gifts given out of faith and love don't just land in some church bank account; they are deposited straight into God's own treasury. And He pays them back in heavenly goods. And not according to the world's standards (where everything is measured by "How much?"), but according to heaven's generous standard.

Jesus (through the gospel writers) has made a poor widow's tiny offering famous forever. With His smile of approval, that little gift has shone through the centuries brighter than any gold coin ever could. It has blessed countless people by the powerful lesson it teaches.

It says to you: Your smallest 'farthing' - your gift—if it's truly all you can give, and if it's given honestly from the heart (the way every one of us should give to the Lord)—carries His full approval, His special stamp, and His everlasting blessing.

If we would only pause more often, quietly asking the Holy Spirit to help us picture Jesus Himself running heaven's treasury—personally marking every sincere gift and then using it to build His kingdom—our money would start to glow with a whole new brilliance in our eyes.

We'd also begin to say: "The less I spend on myself and the more I give to my Lord, the richer I really am."

And we'd discover the same truth the widow lived: she was far richer in her giving and in the grace she received than all the wealthy people who gave big amounts.

In the same way, the richest person of all is the one who truly and joyfully gives everything they possibly can.

4. Money giving a continual help on the ladder to heaven.

You know how often Jesus talked about money in His parables—He kept coming back to it because it matters so much.

In the story of the shrewd manager, He said: "Use worldly wealth to make friends for yourselves, so that when it's gone, you will be welcomed into eternal homes."

In the parable of the talents, He said to the servant 'you ought to have put my money to use.' The person who had not used his money, lost everything.

In the picture of the sheep and the goats, the ones who hear "Come, you who are blessed by My Father, inherit the kingdom" are the very ones who fed the hungry, clothed the naked, and cared for the broken—in His name.

We can't buy our way into heaven—no amount of money or good deeds can do that.

But when we give money generously, something powerful happens inside us: our hearts become more heavenly-minded, our love for Christ deepens, our compassion for people grows, and our devotion to God's work is both nurtured and proven.

One day we'll hear Jesus say, "Come, you who are blessed by My Father—inherit the kingdom," and yes, He will take into account what we did with the money He gave us—how much of it we truly spent on Him and on the things close to His heart.

In that sense, our giving is part of what gets us ready for heaven.

So many people would happily write a huge check if it could purchase holiness or a guaranteed place in heaven. It can't. No money can buy those.

But here's what they don't realize: when we give generously, sacrificially, out of love and faith in the One who paid everything for us, that very act powerfully moves us along the road to holiness and draws heaven closer. It carries an amazing, eternal reward.

So keep giving day after day—as God provides and as He leads. Each gift makes heaven feel nearer to you, and it brings you nearer to heaven.

The same Jesus who once sat watching people put their offerings into the temple treasury is still my Jesus today.

He sees every gift I give.

Anything offered with wholehearted devotion and love He gladly accepts.

He trains His disciples to judge as he judges and value gifts the way He does, and He will teach me personally—how much to give, how lovingly, how honestly.

Of all the things I want to learn from Him, money is at the top of the list.

Money—so often the source of temptation, sin, heartbreak, and even eternal ruin—can, when I receive it, manage it, and give it away at the feet of Jesus, the true Owner of everything, become one of God's most amazing ways to allow me to spiritually grow and bless others.

In this area too, we are more than conquerors through Him who loved us.

Lord, give Your church—and every one of us—the same heart that poor widow had.

PART 2
THE HOLY SPIRIT AND MONEY

When the Holy Spirit came down at Pentecost to live inside believers, He took complete charge of their whole lives. They were no longer to do or be anything except under His direct inspiration and leading. In everything they were to move and live and have their being "in the Spirit," - to be wholly spiritual people.

That naturally included their possessions, their property, and especially their money—how they earned it and how they spent it. They came under the Spirit's rule too.

Everything about their income and spending was now governed by brand-new, heavenly principles that were not known before.

We see more than one proof of this in the first chapters of Acts. Proof of the all-embracing claim of the Holy Spirit to guide and judge disciples in the disposal of money.

If I really want to know, as a Christian, how we're supposed to handle money and how to give, the best place to learn is right here—what the Holy Spirit Himself taught the very first church about money.

LESSON 1

First we have: **THE HOLY SPIRIT TAKES POSSESSION OF THE MONEY.**

"All the believers were together and had everything in common. They sold property and possessions and shared the money with those in need" (Acts 2:44–45).

Later we read: "Those who owned land or houses sold them, brought the money from the sales and put it at the apostles' feet… Barnabas, for example, sold a field he owned and brought the money and put it at the apostles' feet" (Acts 4:34–37).

Money

No one commanded them to do this. No rule was laid down. It simply happened—spontaneously, joyfully—because the Holy Spirit had filled their hearts with God's love and with the overwhelming reality of heavenly riches. In that overflowing joy they gladly let go of their possessions and put everything at the Lord's disposal through His servants.

It would actually have been strange if things had been any different—and it would have been a terrible loss for the church.

Money is the great symbol of this world's power and happiness. It is one of its strongest idols, constantly pulling people away from God and tempting them into worldly living. A salvation that didn't completely free us from money's grip would not be full salvation.

The story of Pentecost proves that when the Holy Spirit comes in His fullness and fills a heart, earthly possessions lose their hold.

Mone is only valued as a means of proving our love and doing service to our Lord and our fellow men.

The same fire that consumes the sacrifice on the altar also turns our money into "altar gold"—set apart, holy to the Lord.

Here is the real secret of truly Christian giving (and actually of all truly Christian living): the joy of the Holy Spirit.

So much of our giving today lacks this joy. We give out of habit, because others expect it or persuade us, because it's our duty, or because we feel sorry for people in need. It has more to do with us being charitable than the power and the love of the Holy Spirit.

Those motives aren't wrong in themselves —the Holy Spirit can use them to stir us. We do need clear principles and steady habits of giving. But none of that is enough. If our gifts are going to be a "sweet-smelling sacrifice" that pleases God and truly blesses our own souls, they must flow from the joy

Money

and love that only the Holy Spirit can pour into our hearts.

The secret of true giving is the joy of the Holy Spirit.

The constant complaint in the church—how desperately short of money we are for God's work, how shockingly little God's people give compared to what they spend on themselves—is heard everywhere. The heartbroken pleas of pastors and missionaries who work among the poor and the lost are heart-piercing.

Let's be honest: this is clear proof that most believers today know very little of the Holy Spirit's full power in their lives.

So let's pray fervently and earnestly that our whole life may be so lived in the joy of the Holy Spirit—a life so completely surrendered to His control—so that everything we give becomes a spiritual sacrifice offered through Jesus Christ.

LESSON 2

THE HOLY SPIRIT CAN WORK PERFECTLY WELL WITHOUT MONEY.

Our second Pentecostal lesson on money is found in Acts 3:6:

Peter said to the crippled man, "Silver or gold I do not have, but what I do have I give you. In the name of Jesus Christ of Nazareth, walk!"

Here it is: the Holy Spirit showing He can work perfectly well without money.

Our first lesson was that the Spirit-filled church of Pentecost needs money for its work —and the Holy Spirit provides it. Abundant, joyful giving can be one of the clearest signs that the Spirit is moving mightily and powerfully. Money is a blessed means of opening the way for His fuller action.

But there's a danger: people start thinking money is the main thing, that lots of money coming in proves the Spirit is at work, that money itself is the church's strength and blessing.

Our second lesson destroys that illusion. It teaches us that the Holy Spirit's power can shine just as brightly—often even more brightly—when there is no money at all.

The Holy Spirit is is the mighty power of God, and sometimes He uses His people's money, and sometimes He shows how divinely independent He is of it.

The church must hold both truths at once: the Holy Spirit claims every cent we have, yet His mightiest works can be done without a single coin. The church must never beg for money as though cash were the secret of our strength.

Look at the apostles Peter and John—penniless, yet because of that very poverty they were free to give heavenly riches. "Poor, yet making many rich."

They had learned this from Jesus Himself. Peter says, "Silver and gold have I none; in the name of Jesus Christ, walk."

Jesus had taught them to live without money, a poverty resting on trusting the Father completely. He set them a wonderful example. By His own holy poverty, Jesus proved to people that a life of perfect trust and total dependence on the Father makes earthly things irrelevant. That living a life of earthly poverty enables a person to carry and give away eternal treasure easier.

The inner circle of His disciples found in following the footsteps of His poverty the fellowship of His power.

The apostle Paul learned the same lesson from the Holy Spirit: that staying completely detached from material things—even from those things that are allowed for a Christian—is a wonderful, and he almost appears to say essential, help in witnessing the absolute reality of unseen, heavenly riches. And to show they are absolutely enough.

We can be sure that as the Holy Spirit

moves in power in His church, we will see both sides again - there will again be seen His mighty operation in the possession of His people.

- Some believers will once again in their giving make themselves poor, so convinced are they of the surpassing worth of their heavenly inheritance and because they are so filled with the Spirit's joy.

- Others, who are poor and struggling in God's work, will learn to live and walk with a fresh joyful confidence: "Silver and gold I have none—but what I have I give you: in the name of Jesus, walk!"

- And some, who are not called to give away everything, will still give with a freedom and generousness that the world has never seen. They will do this because they have tasted the privilege of total surrender and want to come as close to living this as they can.

Then we will have a church that gives

freely and abundantly, yet never for a moment trusting in its bank balance—instead honoring most highly those who, like Jesus, have the spiritual maturity and strength to joyfully embrace poverty for the sake of the kingdom. A church that becomes imitators of Christ in His poverty.

LESSON 3

Our third lesson is: **THE HOLY SPIRIT TESTS THE MONEY.**

All the money that is given, even in a time when the Holy Spirit is moving mightily, is not always given under His inspiration. But the money is all given under His holy supervision, and He will from time to time, to each heart that honestly yields to Him, reveal what there may be lacking or wrong.

Barnabas sold a field and brought all the money. But Ananias sold a piece of property but secretly kept back part of the price. He

Money

brought the rest and laid it at the apostles' feet—pretending it was the full amount. He and his wife died for that lie - smitten dead.

What made his gift so deadly was that he pretended to give everything when he was actually holding some back. He was a deceitful giver. He gave with half a heart and wanted the praise for total sacrifice while making only a partial sacrifice,

In the Spirit-filled church at Pentecost, the giving was inspired by the Holy Spirit; Ananias' lie was therefore a direct sin against the Holy Spirit Himself.

No wonder that it is written twice that great fear gripped the whole church.

If it's that easy to sin even while giving, and if the Holy Spirit watches and judges every gift, we have every reason to be careful and to fear God.

The heart of Ananias' sin was simple: he did not give what he claimed to give. That same spirit—though usually more subtle—is far more common than we like to admit.

Many Christians say they have given their all to God, yet the way they spend their money proves the words are not true. They claim to be stewards, holding everything for the Lord to direct—yet the tiny fraction they give to God's work compared to what they keep for themselves and accumulating for their future security shows that 'stewardship' is just a nicer word for their own ownership.

We may not be guilty of crucifying Jesus the way Judas, Caiaphas, or Pilate were, but we can still share the same self-serving spirit. We can grieve the Holy Spirit while outwardly condemning Ananias—by holding back what we have promised to give God.

The only protection is honest, reverent fear of ourselves and a total willingness to let the Holy Spirit examine every thought, every excuse, every calculation about how much we "can afford" to keep or give. Our giving must be done in His light if it is to be done in His joy.

What probably led Ananias into sin? Most likely the example of Barnabas and the desire not to look less generous. How often do we give because we're afraid of what people will think if we don't? We care more about human opinion than about God's judgment. We forget that God measures gifts only by what the heart truly gives. Only the wholehearted giver meets His smile.

May the Holy Spirit teach us to make every gift part and parcel of a life completely consecrated to God. That can only happen when we are filled with the Holy Spirit—and this can happen for God longs to fill us with his spirit.

LESSON 4

4. THE HOLY SPIRIT CAN REJECT MONEY ALTOGETHER.

There is another lesson, no less important, no less serious than that of Ananias (Acts 8. 19). The Holy Ghost rejecting Money.

Simon the sorcerer saw the power at work through the apostles and offered them money, saying, "Give me this power too." But Peter replied, "May your money perish with you, because you thought you could buy the gift of God with it!" (Acts 8:19–20).

Trying to buy spiritual power or position in God's church with money brings destruction.

Here, more than with Ananias, it was simple ignorance of the spiritual and unworldly character of the Kingdom of Christ. Simon the sorcerer simply didn't understand the nature of Christ's kingdom. How little Simon understood the men he dealt with.

The apostles needed money. They could have used the cash for themselves or others—but the Holy Spirit, with the powers and the treasures of the unseen world, had so completely filled them, had so possessed them, that money was as if nothing to them.

Better that Simon's money perish than that it have any say in the church of God. Better that it perish than that anyone imagine for one moment that a rich man can buy a place or influence or power that a poor man cannot have.

Has the church throughout history always been faithful to this principle, protesting the claims of wealth? Sadly, no. There have been noble exceptions—true apostolic succession following the giving of the gift of God without consideration of earthly things—but far too often, the rich have been given honor and influence simply because of their money, and not because of spiritual character or godliness. That has surely grieved the Spirit and hurt the church.

For us personally, the danger is real and it's really important for us to be aware of that.

Our natural, fleshly way of thinking (with all its ingrained attitudes, habits, and feelings) is so shaped by the spirit of this world and by our flesh that only a deep, constant filling with the Holy Spirit can free us from money's spell.

Only He can make us completely dead to worldly ways of thinking about wealth and power. And He can only give it as He fills us with the very presence and power of the life of God.

Let us pray for such a strong faith in the surpassing greatness and all-sufficiency of the Holy Spirit—God's supreme gift to His church to be her strength and riches—that money is always kept firmly under Christ's feet and under ours, recognized and valued only as a tool for His heavenly ministry.

Blessed Lord Jesus,

Teach us and help us to always be like Barnabas, to lay all our money at Your feet and hold it entirely at Your disposal;

Money

Teach us and help us to always be like Peter, to rejoice in the poverty that teaches us to prove our trust in the power of Your Spirit;

Teach us and help us to not ever be like Ananias—making a show of total devotion while secretly holding back in our giving;

Teach us and help us not to act like Simon, imagining that Your gifts or influence over people can be bought with money.

Most blessed Holy Spirit, fill us completely. Come and so fill Your church with Your living presence that all our money belongs to You alone.

Andrew Murray

PART 3
THE GRACE OF GOD AND MONEY

> "For you know the grace of our Lord Jesus Christ, that though he was rich, yet for your sakes he became poor, so that you through his poverty might become rich." (2 Corinthians 8:9)

In this and the following chapters we have Paul's teaching on the subject of Christian giving

Paul is talking about arranging a collection from the Gentile Corinthian churches to help the poor Jewish believers in Jerusalem. While doing this, he lifts their eyes to the heavenly value of their earthly money and lays out the principles that should move them - and us - every time we give money in God's service.

He does this especially by pointing to the churches in Macedonia and their astonishing generosity. He makes them into an example that stands for all time. They are living proof of what God's grace can do: making the simple act of collecting money into an occasion of deep joy.

The Macedonians are a true example and clear revelation of true Christ-likeness, and a flood of thanksgiving and glory to God.

Let's note the main lessons. These will help us find the path by which our money can become more and more a channel and a proof that the life of heaven is growing inside us.

1. THE GRACE OF GOD ALWAYS TEACHES US TO GIVE (8:1)

"We make known to you the grace of God which hath been given to the churches of Macedonia."

Over two chapters, the word "grace" appears eight times.

- Once it refers to "the grace of our Lord Jesus Christ," who became poor for our sakes.

- Once it speaks of the grace that God is able to make abound in us.

- The other six times it appears when talking about the specific grace of giving.

We all think we know what grace is. Grace is not only God's kindness toward us; it is the living power He puts inside us—the very force and energy of the Christian life worked in us by the Holy Spirit.

Grace is the force, the power, the energy of the Christian life, as it is wrought in us by the Holy Spirit.

We all know the command to stand firm in grace, to grow in grace, to seek for more grace—abounding grace, super-abounding grace, exceedingly abundant grace. We rejoice in the words and pray continually, constantly asking God to increase and magnify His grace in us.

Money

Here is a fixed law of the Christian life: no grace - no spiritual gift - can be truly known or increased unless we actually live it out.

So learn this: one of the chief ways God's grace, God's power, God's fullness, is expressed and strengthened in us is by us using our money to help others.

The reason is clear. Grace in God is His free, overflowing compassion toward the undeserving. His grace is free. Grace delights to always give, with no thought of whether the receiver deserves the gift.

God's very life and joy is in giving. When that same grace enters our hearts, it keeps its nature (it cannot change): whether in God or in us, grace loves to give and rejoices in giving.

Grace teaches people to see money the way God sees it: its main value, its God-like power, is the ability to do good—even if it means we become poorer so that someone else can become richer.

We should learn the lessons:

• If God's grace truly lives in us, it will show itself in giving.
• If we want fresh grace and more grace, we must exercise the grace we already have—by giving.
• Every time we give, we should do it with the conscious awareness that this is God's own grace working in us and through us.

2. THE GRACE OF GOD TEACHES US TO GIVE GENEROUSLY (8:2–4)

"Their deep poverty abounded unto the riches of their liberality, for according to their power, yea, beyond their power, they gave of their own accord, beseeching us with much entreaty in regard of this grace."

What a sight! And what a proof of the power of grace!

These newly converted Gentiles in

Money

Macedonia hear about the desperate needs of Jewish believers in Jerusalem—people they have never met, people they once looked down on —and instantly, they want to help and share with them what they have.

They of their own choosing give far beyond their means. Paul actually tries to refuse their gifts because they are so poor; but they beg him with passionate pleading until he finally accepts.

"Their deep poverty abounded unto the riches of their liberality."

It is a remarkable fact that poor people are almost always more generous than the rich. They do not cling so tightly to what they have. They more easily part with what they have. The deceitfulness of the love of money has not hardened their hearts. They have learned to trust God for tomorrow.

The world looks at them and says, "It costs them nothing to give everything; they are used to having little." But that is exactly what makes their giving so precious to God: it flows from a simple, childlike heart that has never learned the habit of hoarding and holding on.

This is how God's kingdom of grace on earth always works: from below upward.

"Not many wise and not many noble are called. God has chosen the weak and the base things." (1 Corinthians 1:26–28).

In the same way He has chosen the poor of this world, who out of their deep poverty give so freely, to teach the rich what true generosity really looks like.

"Far beyond their power gave they of their own accord, beseeching us with much entreaty that we would receive the gift."

Imagine if this Macedonian spirit swept through our churches today—if believers of modest means and believers with great wealth joined the poor in adopting this same standard of giving.

If the Macedonian example became the

law of Christian generosity, money would pour into the work of God's kingdom in ways we can hardly dream of.

3. THE GRACE OF GOD TEACHES US TO GIVE JOYFULLY.

"The abundance of their joy abounded unto the riches of their liberality." (v. 2.)

In the Christian life, joy is the clear sign of health and whole-hearted commitment.

Joy is not just something we feel now and then; it's the constant proof that we are experiencing and enjoying the Savior's love. Joy is meant to fill not only our spiritual moments but also our everyday tasks and our hardest trials— "a joy that no man taketh from you."

And so joy inspires our giving. It turns the act of offering our money into a sacrifice of joy and thanksgiving. When we give with joy, that very act becomes a fresh source of joy for us, because we are sharing in the joy of the One who said, "It is more blessed to give than to receive."

Oh, the happiness of giving! If only people truly believed how certain and sure this path is to never-ending joy—to keep on giving, just as God lives to give.

When Israel brought their gifts for the temple, we read, "then the people rejoiced, because with a perfect heart they offered willingly to the Lord; and David the King also rejoiced with great joy."

That's a joy we can carry through every day of our lives—constantly and unceasingly sharing our gifts of money, our time, our lives, our service all around us.

God has planted the desire for happiness deep in every heart; the heart cannot help being drawn to what truly brings happiness.

Let's fill our hearts with the conviction that giving brings joy. That joy will make our calls to give—whether we're rich or poor—one of our most treasured privileges as a believer.

Then it will be true of us: "and the abundance of their joy abounded to the riches of their liberality."

4. The grace of God makes our giving part of our surrender to our Lord (v. 5)

Paul says of the Macedonians' giving (v. 5), they not only did this, "but first they gave themselves to the Lord."

In this one sentence we have one of the most beautiful descriptions of what true salvation requires—and what full salvation really is.

A person who has given themselves completely to the Lord: that covers everything God asks of us as He will handle all the rest. This phrase appears nowhere else in Scripture; we owe it to Paul's teaching here about this offering.

It shows us that giving money means nothing unless we have first given ourselves.

It shows us that every act of giving must simply be a fresh renewal and expression of that first great surrender of our whole selves.

It shows us that each new gift of money can become a beautiful reminder and renewal of the joy of being totally set apart for God - of being consecrated to Him.

Only this truth can lift our giving above the routine level of ordinary Christian duty and make it a true expression and strengthening of God's grace in us.

We are not under law, but under grace. Yet so much of our giving—whether in the church offering plate, on a pledge card, or for special causes—is done automatically, without any real direct connection to our Lord.

A truly consecrated life is one lived moment by moment in His love. It is this kind of life that will help us do what seems so hard, which is to always give in the right spirit. This giving is done as an act of true worship. It is this that will make "the abundance of our joy abound to the riches of our liberality."

5. THE GRACE OF GOD MAKES OUR GIVING PART OF THE CHRISTLIKE LIFE (V. 9)

"See that ye abound in this grace also, for ye know the grace of our Lord Jesus Christ, that though He was rich, yet for our sakes He became poor."

Every branch, leaf, and flower of the mightiest oak tree draws its life from the same strong root that supports the trunk. The life in the tiniest bud is the same life that's in the strongest branch.

We are branches in Christ, the Living Vine; we share the very same life that lived and worked in Him. How important it is that we truly understand His life, so we can willingly and intelligently yield to it.

Here Paul reveals one of its deepest roots: "Though he was rich, yet for your sakes he became poor, that ye through His poverty might become rich."

To make us rich and bless us, Christ made Himself poor. That's why the widow's tiny offering pleased Him so much: her gift matched His own generous measure—"She cast in all she had."

This is the life, grace and power He wants to work in us; there is no other pattern, no other mould for the Christ-life.

"See that ye abound in this grace also; for ye know the grace of our Lord Jesus, that he became poor."

How little those Macedonian Christians realized that in their deep poverty and overflowing generosity—giving far beyond what they could afford—they were simply living out the Spirit and grace of Jesus working in them.

How surprising that the simple gifts of these poor people became the basis for such profound, high and holy, and heart-searching teaching.

How much we need to pray that the Holy Spirit would so take control of our wallets and our possessions that our way of giving truly reflects—however imperfectly—the grace and giving of our Lord.

And how we need to bring our giving to the foot of the cross, seeking the power of Christ's death to the world and its riches to become our power too. Then we will make others rich through our poverty, and our lives will echo Paul's words: "poor, yet making many rich."

6. GOD'S GRACE - GOD'S POWER IN US - DOESN'T JUST MAKE US WANT TO GIVE; IT ACTUALLY MAKES US DO IT. (V. 10.)

"You were the first to make a beginning a

year ago, not only to do, but also to will. But now complete the doing also; that as there was the readiness to will, so there may be the performance also."

We all know how huge the gap can be between wanting to do something and actually doing it. And this applies to us giving money too.

- Some of us keep telling ourselves, "When I'm making more money, I'll be generous then." Meanwhile that daydream deceives them and becomes an excuse for not being generous right now.

- Others have the cash sitting there and keep meaning to do something generous with it, yet they hesitate and years roll by and it never happens.

- Plenty of us feel pretty good about ourselves and think we are generous because of what we say about what we'd like to do with our money (that is what we will to do), when the truth is in what we do in practice -

we're not even giving generously out of what we have today. This is not what God would love to see.

Paul's message hits us: "Now finish the doing!"

"Now complete the doing also; that as the readiness to will, so the completion also, out of your ability."

"It is God which worketh in us to will and to do". (Philippians 2:13).

God is the One who puts both the desire and the power to act inside us. So let's not block Him with unbelief, disobedience or laziness and just camp out on the will - the wanting part without going on to the to do.

The Christian life needs action—it is by acting that godliness grows.

If you look at your giving and realize it's fallen short of the joyful, surrendered, sacrificial pattern we see in Scripture, if it's not as generous and joyful, if it's not done in the spirit of absolute surrender to Jesus or of following His example of making Himself poor for us, then, add the doing to the wanting, right now.

7. GOD'S GRACE MAKES EVERY GIFT ACCEPTABLE BASED ON WHAT SOMEONE HAS. (V. 12)

"For if the readiness is there, it is acceptable according as a man hath, not according as he hath not."

God looks straight at the heart and measures your gift against your actual ability. And His Spirit whispers back to an honest heart, "Yes—this one pleased the Father." God has been careful to teach us this in His Word in every possible way.

Heaven's whole value system flips the world's upside down: the love that gives generously, that stretches what you do have, is met with the Father's delighted love pouring down from above.

So let's stop giving the norm that let's feel okay about ourselves and we think is enough. Let's stop giving the expected. Let's pause and rejoice in the call to give. Let's rejoice in His Spirit who shows us what and how much to give, and then watch the deep joy of giving hit us—because the Spirit puts His own seal on it: the Father is well pleased.

8. GOD'S GRACE USES GIVING TO CREATE REAL EQUALITY AND ONENESS AMONG ALL BELIEVERS. (V. 13–15)

"I say not this, that others may be eased and ye distressed; but by equality, your abundance being a supply at this present time for their want, that their abundance may also become a supply to your want. That there may be equality. As it is written: He that gathered much, had nothing over: and he that gathered little had no lack."

Another ray of heavenly light on this

appeal for a collection: Money becomes the cable that ties the church together into one.

Jerusalem believers and Corinth believers —total strangers, different cultures, Jews and Gentiles in Christ—become one body because love and cash flow between them.

They are one as much as Israel was one people. Just as when Israel gathered manna, the weak and the strong were all told to bring everything into one common store so that everyone ended up with exactly what they needed, so it is in the body of Christ.

God deliberately allows some to be rich and others to be poor; He hands out His gifts in ways that look uneven, precisely so that our love can have the high privilege of stepping in and restoring real equality.

Others needs are God's call to us. A call to step in with love and practical help, and receive the deep blessing that comes with giving to others.

And then, at another time or in another

area of life, the very people who once needed help may find themselves with plenty—and they, in turn, can pour out blessing from their abundance upon their helpers.

Everything has been arranged by God this way on purpose: so that love always has room to move, and so that we constantly get fresh chances to grow into and to prove the Christ-like spirit.

What an urgent call—and what a vast field of needs lay before every one of God's people to prove that we have truly made God's plan our own. The plan "that there may be equality," and that the selfish, "I've got mine" attitude that clings to privilege has been nailed to the cross and killed.

In charitable works and in world missions, how desperately we need every believer to do their absolute utmost—"according to their power—yea, and beyond their power."

When the world looks at the church, they ought to see a family where no one hoards and everyone shares so that there really is fairness.

When the unreached nations look at us, what a heart-piercing cry rises up: that there would finally be real equality, that we who have so much in Christ would truly share and share alike with them everything God has given us.

In that moment, money suddenly takes on a breathtaking, eternal value we never imagined: it becomes one of the greatest tools we have to pour the overflowing riches we possess in Christ into the hands of those who are perishing without him.

There is no room left to enlarge on the further lessons of Chapter 9. Let me just briefly mention them:

- **v. 6:** Give generously and you'll receive generously from God.
- **v. 7:** Don't give reluctantly or because you feel pressured—God loves the person

who gives with a big smile.

• **v. 8:** Give boldly and in faith—God will make every kind of grace overflow to you.

• **v. 11–13:** Your generosity makes people thank God and praise Him and so brings glory to God.

• **v. 15:** Every gift you give points back to God's indescribable gift—Jesus—and fills hearts with thanks for this.

The gifts of those poor Macedonians and the Corinthian believers open up a whole universe of heavenly truth and light! Can we let that light shine on our own wallets and bank accounts right now? Can we look again at everything we're spending on ourselves and ask, "Is this in line with the pattern Paul lays out here?"

Let's do it today—hand over to the One who became poor for us everything that self-interest and self-indulgence have been clinging to.

Andrew Murray

Let's beg Him to show us, by His Spirit, that the only real value money has is to spend it on our Lord, to bless people, to use it as a workout for grace, and to turn even our cash into treasure that will last forever.

PART 4
THE POVERTY OF CHRIST

"Ye know the grace of our Lord Jesus Christ, that, though He was rich, yet for your sakes He became poor, that ye through His poverty might become rich." (2 Corinthians 8:9)

"Through his poverty"—what does that really mean?

Did it mean that He stripped himself of every heavenly and earthly possession so that the riches of earth and heaven could be ours?

Did it mean that He stepped into our place and walked the path of earthly poverty so that we, in comfort and ease, could enjoy the heavenly riches He has won for us?

Or does "THROUGH HIS POVERTY" carry a deeper meaning? Does it imply that

His poverty is the very path or passage that He opened up, and that everyone who wants to enter fully into His riches must walk through it?

Does it mean that, just as He had to become poor in spirit and in body, dying to the world in order to open the way to heavenly treasures for us, so we too must imitate Him, walking in His footsteps, and only through His poverty working in us, through real fellowship with His poverty, can we come to the full enjoyment of the riches he came to bring?

In other words, is the poverty of Jesus something for Him alone, or is it something His disciples are meant to share?

There is hardly a single trait in the life and character of Christ that we do not look to as an example. What, then, are the lessons His holy poverty has to teach us?

Is the right to own and enjoy the riches of this earth, as it is now practiced almost everywhere in the church, truly part of what Christ secured for us?

Or could it be that our lack of faith in the beauty and blessedness of the poor life of Christ Jesus is one of the reasons for our spiritual poverty? That our refusal to share Christ's poverty is the reason we lack his riches?

Is there not an urgent need for us to think not only of the words "for your sakes he became poor," but just as much of the words "for his sake I suffer the loss of all things"?

In searching for an answer to these questions, we must first turn and fix our eyes on our blessed Lord, waiting in prayer for the Holy Spirit to reveal something of the glory of this wonderful character trait of His.

Unless our heart is fixed on Him in patient, prayerful gazing, and unless we wait for the Holy Spirit to give us His light, we may have thoughts about this divine poverty, but we will never truly see its glory or let its power and blessing enter our lives. May God give us understanding!

We must first see why there was a divine necessity for the earthly poverty of Christ.

He could have lived on earth as a rich man, giving away money with wisdom and generosity.

He could have had a modest income, just enough to keep Him from the homelessness and need that marked His life and was His lot.

In either case, He could have taught His people in every age priceless lessons about the right use of this world's goods. What a sermon His life would have been on the words "those who buy something, as if it did not belong to them."

But no, there was a divine must that his life be one of complete poverty.

In looking for the explanation for this, we find two classes of reasons.

There are reasons that relate to us and to

Christ's work as our Saviour.

There are other reasons that are more closely tied to His own personal life as a man and to the work the Father did in Him as he was perfected through suffering.

Of the reasons that concern His work for us, the main ones are easy to name.

Christ's poverty is part of his total self-emptying, a proof of His perfect humility, his willingness to go down to the very lowest depths of human misery and share fully in all the consequences of sin.

The poor have over all ages always been despised, while the rich have always been courted and honored: Christ came to be despised and rejected in this way too.

Christ's poverty has always been seen as one of the greatest proofs of his love. Love delights to give; perfect love gives everything.

Christ's poverty is one of the clearest expressions of that self-sacrificing love that held nothing back and seeks to win us by the most complete self-denial on our behalf.

Christ's poverty makes Him perfectly fit to sympathize with us and help us in all the trials that come from our relationship with this world and its goods.

Most of mankind has always struggled with poverty. Most of God's saints have been poor and afflicted.

Christ's poverty has assured tens of thousands of people that He truly understands them, that earthly need can become the school of faith, and that God's faithfulness turns lack into the path to heavenly riches.

Christ's poverty is the weapon and the proof of His complete victory over the world. As our Redeemer, He showed by His poverty that His kingdom is not of this world, that He could be tempted neither by its threats nor by its wealth.

But all these reasons are more outward

and official. The deeper spiritual meaning of Christ's poverty becomes clear when we see it as part of His training as the Son of Man, as part of His revelation of what true human life is meant to be.

Christ's poverty was part of the suffering through which He learned obedience and was made perfect by God as our High Priest.

Poverty is always a trial to human nature. We were created to be kings and to rule over and own everything. Having nothing causes us real suffering.

Christ's human nature was not a mere appearance as the Docetæ taught - [an early Christian heresy- Ed]

> [Docetæ (or Docetists (from the Greek word δοκεῖν / dokein = "to seem" or "to appear") were an early Christian heresy (mainly 1st–3rd centuries) that taught:
>
> Jesus only seemed to have a real human body and only seemed to suffer and die on the cross.

They believed that Christ was a purely spiritual/divine being who took on the appearance of a man, but never truly became flesh, never truly felt hunger, pain, or death. In their view, the incarnation, physical suffering, and crucifixion were illusions or mere appearances.

The early church rejected Docetism as dangerous because:

It denies the full humanity of Jesus ("true man of true man").

It undermines the reality of the cross and the atonement (if he only "seemed" to die, he didn't actually pay for our sins).

It contradicts clear Scripture (e.g., John 1:14 "the Word became flesh"; 1 John 4:2–3; 2 John 7).

That's why Andrew Murray stresses that Jesus' human nature was not a mere appearance: he genuinely experienced poverty, hunger, contempt, and suffering as a real man. His poverty (and ours in following him) is therefore real and meaningful, not illusory.]

Money

No one has ever been more truly and intensely human than Jesus Christ: true man of true man.

Poverty means dependence on others; it means contempt and shame; it often means hunger and pain; it always means lacking the money and power of this world. Our blessed Lord felt all of this as a man.

It was part of the suffering through which the Father worked out His purpose in the Son, and the Son proved His submission to the Father and His absolute trust in him.

Christ's poverty was part of His school of faith, where He himself first learned, and then taught the world, that life is more than food and that man lives "not by bread alone, but by every word that proceeds from the mouth of God."

In His own life, he proved that God and the riches of heaven can completely satisfy a person who has nothing on earth, that trusting God for daily needs is never in vain, and that we only ever need what God chooses to give.

In His person, we have living proof that the preaching of the kingdom of heaven carries power when the preacher Himself shows as proof that the kingdom is enough.

Christ's poverty was one of the clearest marks of His total separation from the world, proof that He belonged to another world and another spirit.

Sin entered the world through the desire for what looked good and was pleasing to the eye (the apple in Eden); the world's greatest power over people lies in the cares, possessions, and pleasures of this life.

Christ came to conquer the world, to drive out its prince, and to win the world back to God.

He did it by refusing every temptation to accept the world's gifts or seek its help.

His poverty was one of the strongest parts of his protest against the spirit of this world, its self-pleasing, and its trust in what can be seen and is material.

He overcame the world first in the temptations the prince of this world used against Him, and then, through that victory, overcame its power over us.

The poverty of Christ was therefore no accident or external detail. It was an essential part of His holy, perfect life, one of the great secrets of His power to conquer and to save, His path to the glory of God.

We want to know what our share in the poverty of Christ is supposed to be, whether and how far we are to follow His example. Let us look at what Christ taught His disciples.

When He said to them, "Follow me," "Come after me and I will make you fishers of men," He was calling them to share his poor and homeless life, to live in complete dependence on the Father's care and on the kindness of people.

He more than once used strong words about forsaking all, renouncing everything, losing everything.

And they understood him: they left their boats and tax booths, and Peter could say, "We have left everything to follow you."

Jesus' call to "come after me" is often treated as if it were simply the call to repentance and salvation. That is not the case.

The principles behind the call apply to all believers, but to understand and apply them rightly we must first see what the call originally meant.

Christ gathered a group of men who were to live with him in the closest possible fellowship, in complete conformity to His life, under His direct training.

These three things were essential if they were to receive the Holy Spirit and become true witnesses to Him and to the life He lived and would give to others.

Money

For them, just as for him, surrendering all possessions and accepting a life of poverty was clearly a necessary condition and means by which they could receive the full heavenly riches with power to convince the world of their reality.

With Paul, the picture is hardly different. Without any recorded command, the Spirit of his Master so filled him and made the unseen world so real and glorious that earthly property and position simply lost all meaning.

He was able to say, as no one else ever could, words that must have reflected the deepest heart of our Lord: "as poor, yet making many rich; as having nothing, yet possessing all things."

In his wonderful life and his letters, Paul shows the weight that a testimony about eternal things carries when the witness can point to his own experience of the complete satisfaction the unseen riches give.

In Paul, as in Christ, poverty was the natural result of an all-consuming passion and made him a channel through which the Invisible Power could flow freely.

The history of the church tells a sad story of growing wealth and worldly power and a corresponding loss of the heavenly gift she was meant to share with the nations.

The contrast with the apostolic church is made painfully clear in the story of Thomas Aquinas visiting Rome. When he expressed amazement at the wealth he saw, the Pope said, "We can no longer say with Peter, 'Silver and gold have I none.'"

"No," replied Aquinas, "and neither can we say, 'In the name of Jesus Christ of Nazareth, rise up and walk!'"

Earthly poverty and heavenly power had been closely joined; when one left, the other left too.

Through the centuries the conviction kept returning that only a return to poverty could break the chains of this world and bring back the blessing from above.

Many earnest attempts were made to restore poverty to the place it had in the early church, but again and again the terrible power of the world prevailed.

One reason for the failure was that people did not understand that in Christianity it is never the outward act or condition that matters, but only the spirit that fills it.

They forgot Christ's words, "The kingdom of God is within you," and expected poverty itself to do what only the Spirit of Christ living in poverty can accomplish.

They turned it into laws and monastic rules, forcing souls who had no inner calling into a way of life they were never meant for.

The church clothed poverty with a special holiness and taught the doctrine of "Counsels of Perfection," saying that while the commands of the gospel were for all, certain acts or modes of living were optional and were left to the choice of the disciple to earn extra merit.

These things were not a binding obligation it lied; to follow these Counsels was more than simple obedience, it was a work of supererogation which had special merit.

Out of this grew the idea that the church could distribute the surplus merit of the saints. In some cases, poverty became just another form of self-righteousness, making deals with wealth and casting a dark and deadly shadow over the very people it promised to save.

> [This is talking about how the medieval Catholic system of "works of supererogation" and "the treasury of merit" went badly wrong.
>
> The church taught that the saints in the Bible had done way more good works than were strictly necessary to earn their own salvation. All those "extra" good deeds (especially things

like lifelong poverty, celibacy, martyrdom, etc.) were piled up in a kind of heavenly bank account called the Treasury of Merit.

The church claimed they had the authority to hand out this surplus merit—like spiritual coupons—to ordinary Christians who were short on merit of their own. You could get some of that extra credit by buying indulgences, going on pilgrimage, joining a monastic order, or doing other approved acts.

The result?

Poverty (which was supposed to be a humble following of Jesus) sometimes turned into just another way to rack up merit points. Some people took vows of poverty proudly, thinking "I'm earning treasure in heaven that other people will need to buy from the church later." It stopped being genuine love and became spiritual one-upmanship and self-righteousness.

Even worse, the whole system ended up partnering with wealth instead of challenging it. Rich people who lived in luxury could just pay money (indulgences, donations, funding monasteries) to get a share of the merit that the officially "poor" religious orders had supposedly earned. So poverty and wealth made a dark bargain: the poor looked holy and built up merit, the rich paid cash and got the benefit without having to change their lives.

That's the "covenant with wealth" Murray is talking about: instead of poverty being a prophetic protest against greed, it became part of a machine that actually protected and comforted the greedy. And in the end, the very thing that was meant to lead people to humble dependence on Christ's grace alone ended up casting a "dark and deadly shadow"—keeping people trapped in works-righteousness and away from the true gospel.

That's why Murray says the whole mess discredited the beautiful biblical truth of following Christ in voluntary poverty-Ed.]

At the Reformation, poverty had become so corrupted an idea, that in casting out the Catholic errors, the Reformers threw out much of the truth with the error.

Since then Protestant theology has hardly dared to ask what place, meaning, and power Christ and the Apostle Paul really gave to poverty in their teaching and lives.

Even today, when God is still raising up many witnesses to the joy of giving up everything to trust Him alone, the church has not yet found the right way to express its belief that the spirit of Christ's poverty is still a gift He gives to some of His people.

I have spoken above of the errors connected with the teaching of the Counsels of Perfection. And yet there was a sprinkling of truth in that teaching, too. The error was to say that the highest conformity to Christ was not a matter of duty, but of option. Scripture says, "To him that knoweth to do good and doeth it not, to him it is sin."

Wherever God makes His will clear to someone, that person is obligated to obey it.

The whole error could have been avoided if people had recognized this simple fact: God doesn't reveal the full depth of His will to everyone at the same time or in the same measure. People differ in spiritual insight, maturity, receptivity, gifts, growth, calling, and grace.

That diversity does not change the duty of every single believer to pursue the deepest possible inner likeness to Christ.

What it does change is how fully and

visibly any of us can express that likeness outwardly in the exact same ways Jesus did.

During the three years of His public ministry, Jesus devoted Himself and every minute of His time entirely to the direct work of the Father. He did not earn His own living.

He deliberately chose disciples who would follow Him in that same pattern—leaving jobs, possessions, and security behind so they could give themselves full-time to the work of the Kingdom.

To be part of that inner circle—the ones Jesus hand-picked and trained—He required something He never demanded from the crowds who simply came for healing or salvation.

Those disciples were called to share fully in His mission and, one day, in the glory of the coming Kingdom.

That meant they also had to share fully in His poverty: owning nothing in this world, holding everything in open hands for the Kingdom.

From what has been said above it is clear there is no simple rule that fits everyone.. It is not a question of law, but of liberty.

But we must understand "liberty" correctly. Too often, people talk about Christian freedom as if it mainly means being let off the hook from having to give up too much of our own desires or from having to say no to the pleasures and comforts the world offers.

Its real meaning is the very opposite: it is freedom from self and the world so that we can lovingly give everything to God in spirit and in truth.

Instead of asking, "How much of the world am I still allowed to keep?" the truly free heart asks, "How free am I to follow Christ all the way?"

Among the gifts and callings Christ still gives His church, are there not some whom

His Spirit still draws to bear this part of his image too?

Does the freedom Christ died to give us really mean this: that because we love Him and long to be as close to Him as possible, we are now completely free (free from self, free from the world) to forsake everything and follow Him all the way, even into His poverty?

And among all the gifts and callings He still pours out on His church today, are there not some whom His Spirit still draws (in this very area too) to carry and display the likeness of Christ in His poverty?

Do we not need, just as much as in the days when he and his apostles walked the earth, men and women who give living proof that someone who literally gives up everything earthly because their heart is set on treasure in heaven can still count on God to supply their daily needs?

In a church that everyone admits is

worldly, this is the strongest possible protest against the deadly grip the world has on us.

When people ask why hundreds of millions are spent on luxuries in Christian countries while only a tiny fraction goes to God's work, calculations and arguments about "moderate giving" change almost nothing.

Calculations are made as to what could be done if all Christians were only to be just a little generous, but I fear all such discussion will bring little. Real help must come from another direction.

It was of the inner circle that Jesus gathered around Himself that Christ asked for poverty as absolute and complete as His own.

It is therefore in the innermost circle of God's children, those who claim the deepest insight into grace and the fullest surrender to it, that we must look for the witnesses to show that His Spirit can still enable people to carry

Money

His poverty.

He has done it, and he is still doing it, in missionaries, in Salvation Army workers, in many quiet humble unknown believers.

His Spirit is working out this trait of His blessed likeness. In the days we are looking for in the deeper revival among God's children, He will do it even more.

Blessed are all who wait on Him to receive His teaching, to know His mind, and to show forth His holy likeness.

As the inner circle proves the power of his presence, the second and third outer circles will feel the influence.

People of ordinary means who feel no call to literal poverty will still be gripped by the example and will feel compelled to sacrifice far more comfort than ever before.

The rich will see the danger signs God has placed along their path (Luke 18:25; Matthew 6:19–21; 1 Timothy 6:9–10, 17–19) and, even if they do not share Christ's poverty outwardly, will be helped to set their hearts wholeheartedly on treasure in heaven: being rich in faith, rich in good works, rich toward God, heirs of the riches of his grace and glory.

"That you through his poverty might become rich."

HIS POVERTY, not only as something we believe in, but as something we experience and share, is the door into his richest blessings.

Let us notice some of the ways fellowship with Christ's poverty brings blessing:

What a help it is to the spiritual life! It throws the soul completely on God and the unseen, makes His presence and care real in the smallest details of daily life, and turns simple trust into the heartbeat of every earthly and spiritual need.

Because no one can claim God's supply for daily bread while living in known disobedience, it binds the soul to God's will with the strongest possible tie.

The body's constant needs, instead of being a hindrance, become wonderful aids in lifting the whole of life into fellowship with God and bringing God into everything.

It lifts the spirit above the temporary and teaches contentment, joy, and praise in every circumstance.

What a protest it is against the spirit of this world!

Nothing damages the Christian life more than the subtle worldliness that comes from the cares or the possessions of this life.

This is the Delilah in whose lap the separated Nazarite falls asleep and loses his strength.

To wake the church from that sleep takes more than sermons or ordinary giving that still leaves room for every luxury.

It takes the clear demonstration of the Spirit and power that God can enable people, and make it an unspeakable joy for them, to give up everything earthly, just as their Lord did, so that they can possess, prove, and proclaim the total sufficiency of heavenly riches.

What a doorway it opens into the likeness of Jesus!

We worship our Lord in the form of a servant as the most perfect revelation of humble, self-sacrificing love. His poverty was an inseparable part of that servant-form.

In every age some lovers of Jesus have been unable to rest until they came as close as possible to their beloved Lord in this too.

In Him, the outward and inward were in perfect harmony; one was the only true expression of the other.

In the body of Christ there are many different gifts; the whole body is not eye or ear. So there are some who have the calling and grace to display this part of His image and, for the sake of their brothers and sisters and the watching world, keep alive the memory of this often-neglected side of the incarnation.

Blessed are those whom the Holy Spirit makes representatives of this amazing grace: that though he was rich, yet for our sakes He became poor.

What power it gives to make others rich!

We become rich through his poverty.

When his people live in his poverty, the same blessing flows out.

Many who do not feel called to literal poverty, or whom God in his providence keeps in possessions, are stirred and strengthened by the sight.

The witness of complete surrender moves others to come as close in spirit as they can.

Christian giving becomes not only larger in amount but far more joyful, ready, and sacrificial in spirit.

Through their poverty too, through Christ's poverty in them, many are made rich.

How are we to know what our personal calling is? We can so easily be swayed by ignorance, prejudice, self-indulgence, worldliness, human wisdom, or unbelief, and miss the simple heart that sees God's perfect will.

The safest place is this:

A dying servant of God (the Rev. Geo. Ferguson, the principal of our Mission Institute.) once lay meditating on the promise "Though your sins be as scarlet, they shall be as white as snow."

A voice seemed to ask him:

"Do you know what 'white as snow' means?"

"No, Lord. Only you know."

"Can you make yourself that white?"

"No, Lord, but you can."

"Are you willing for me to do it?"

"Yes, Lord, by your grace I am willing for you to do everything you desire."

Those three questions show us the way

Money

with the poverty of Jesus too.

First: question: Do you know what the heavenly poverty of Jesus really is—what it looked like in Him, in His disciples, in Paul, in His saints through the ages, and what it would look like in you?

Let the honest answer be, "No, Lord. But you know."

That is where we must begin. If God opened our eyes to see the spiritual glory of our Lord in His poverty, His complete renunciation of every earthly comfort and self-pleasing, if we saw how beautiful it is to angels and how pleasing to the Father, we would begin to understand whether we ought to long for it, to desire and imitate it.

Before you judge it, pray that the Holy Spirit will show you the heavenliness and the likeness to Christ it would bring into your life.

Then comes **the second question:** "Can you attain it? Can you, in the likeness of Jesus, give up everything this world offers for God and for your fellowmen, and find your joy only in heavenly riches and in depending completely on God?"

"No, Lord, I cannot, but you can work it in me."

Come and gaze at the Son of God and worship: it was God who made Him what he was, and the same God can, by his mighty power, work His likeness in you.

Ask God to reveal by His spirit what the poverty of Jesus is and then to work in you as much of it as you can receive.

Be sure of this: the deeper you enter His poverty, the richer you will be.

Third, when the heart-searching question comes—"Are you willing for it?"—them surely your answer will be ready: "By your grace, Lord, I am, yes!"

You may see no way out of all the complications of your life. You may dread the sacrifices and trials you cannot bear.

Money

But do not be afraid. You are giving yourself to God's perfect love to work out His perfect will in you.

He will give light and strength for everything He truly asks of you.

The throne of riches, honor, and glory where the Lamb now sits is proof enough that there is no surer road to true riches than the road through His poverty.

The soul that simply says yes to his leading will find that the fellowship of his sufferings is, even here and now, the fellowship of his glory:

"Though He was rich, yet for your sakes He became poor, that ye through His poverty might be rich."

www.ingramcontent.com/pod-product-compliance
Lightning Source LLC
Chambersburg PA
CBHW060339080526
44584CB00013B/843